BIRDS
OF
INDIA

Listen to the chirping of the birds
Without the chirping of the mind!

Osho

A photographic guide to the

BIRDS OF INDIA

including Nepal, Sri Lanka, Bhutan, Pakistan and Bangladesh

text and photography by Amano Samarpan

wisdom
tree

First published 2006
Reprinted July 2006, March 2008

ISBN 81-8328-029-3

Published by
Wisdom Tree
4779/23 Ansari Road
Darya Ganj
New Delhi-110002
Ph: 23247966/67/68

Published by Shobit Arya for Wisdom Tree; *edited by* Manju Gupta;
designed by Kamal P. Jammual; *typeset at* Sai Graphic Design,
New Delhi-110055 and *printed at* Print Perfect, New Delhi-110064

CONTENTS

ACKNOWLEDGEMENTS

To name all the birds in this book and provide descriptions of them was not an easy task. Although inspired by the impeccable observations of Indian birdman Salim Ali, as recorded in his books, I would like to thank contemporary authors for their personal help in species recognition. These include Bikram Grewal and Bill Harvey, Tim and Carol Inskipp as well as Krys Kazmierczak who together are responsible for most of the current popular guide books on Indian birds. Maan Barua of Kaziranga provided valuable editorial help while Eashaan Mahesh assisted with Hindi names. My thanks also go to Barabara Tracy and the many unknown local bird guides and birdwatchers encountered during the decade this book was made.

The first publisher who suggested I did this book was refused. The second publisher bought some scans and set me on my way but was reluctant to publish. My thanks to Shobit Arya of Wisdom Tree for undertaking the task of putting this book into print.

PREFACE

I still remember my first day in India. Lying on a bed in Delhi trying to sleep off jet lag, I was greeted by the sound of House Sparrows outside; after a while, they could be heard inside the room and then I felt them landing on my prone body, using me as one of their perches as they played around. There are not nearly so many House Sparrows in Delhi today yet the gentle wisdom of the *rishi*, sages, and the Buddha seems to have rubbed off on the avian kingdom and I would like to thank all the birds who appear in this book, some of whom were very obliging.

The Clamorous Reed Warbler is one who stands out. Hearing him or her in some undergrowth near the Yamuna river that runs past Delhi, I replied to the tutting sounds coming forth and after a while established a kind of rapport with the little creature until silence fell. It seemed contact was lost until the bird suddenly appeared with a large fly in its mouth, an offering perhaps. Ungratefully, it seemed, I responded with a couple of grab shots before the bird disappeared. After that, although I often heard it, never again did it respond, in spite of my returning the next day and the day after.

It is not easy to define a common bird. One can take into account the actual numbers of the bird (this would limit common to the smaller-sized species), how easy it is to see the bird (larger birds are likely to figure here) or how widespread they are within the region. A combination of these and other factors have been taken into account so that a visitor to the region will be able to identify many of the species he or she sees from this book.

Identification is often something of an art and not the only reason for seeing birds. Often the sheer magnificence of the feathered population and our ability to respond to them is what actually matters.

Amano Samarpan

BIRD TOPOGRAPHY
(the body parts of a bird;
an aid to identification)

Not all the body parts are included here
as ornithologists use many more terms
to scientifically describe a bird.

Nostril

Crown

Forehead

Supercilium

Ear coverts

Nape

Scapulars

Mantle

Back

Rump

Bill, Beak

Mandible

(upper, lower)

Chin

Breast

Lesser Coverts

Median Coverts

Greater Coverts

Belly

Flank

Tail

Vent

Thigh

Tarsus

photo: Bimaculated Lark

Understanding this Book

The birds in this book are mostly widespread, breeding residents although some winter visitors have been included. The taxonomy used is based on *An Annotated Checklist of the Birds of the Oriental Region* by T. Inskipp, N. Lindsey and W. Duckworth (1996) yet reference has also been made to the more recent *Birds of South Asia* by P. Rasmussen and J. Anderton (2005).

English name (top left)
English names have been in common usage ever since the days of modern ornithology in India. However, there is now some disagreement over which names to use, hence more than one may be given. As defined by the International Union for the Conservation of Nature and Natural Resources (IUCN) Red List, *vulnerable* species are marked in red, *near threatened* species in magenta.

Scientific name (in italics below English name)
These names help to identify species more exactly.

Length in centimetres (from tip of beak to end of tail)
The measurements are approximate but give some idea of the size. As a reference, this book is 7.5 inches high (19 cms) by 4.7 inches wide (12 cms).

Hindi name
Some Hindi names are merely alliterations of English ones. There are however genuine Hindi names a few of which come from the Sanskrit language. Other regional names, such as those in Urdu and Bengali, have not been included.

Main photograph
All photographs have been made in the wild (often wildlife parks) with due consideration for the bird's welfare; frightened birds seldom make good photographs!

Text relating to the bird in question
A brief description giving the salient features and habits of the bird concerned.

Area where the bird can be found
Distribution maps are not always accurate, owing to incorrect and missing records while birds do vary in their choice of location particularly in these days of climate change. For areas referred to, see the map at the end of this book.

Other photographs
Many species have subspecies while the birds vary in plumage according to sex, age and the season.

Descriptions of photographs (in italics alongside some photographs)
Helps to further identify the different appearances of a species.

Inhabits dry, open grass and thorny scrub country, avoiding thick forest or humid tracts and is often found near human habitation especially where there is cultivation. Moving in groups that scratch the ground and dung heaps for grain, seed, beetle larvae or termites, it sometimes roosts in trees overnight but usually stays on the ground; although a fast runner, it often flies off with its stubby wings.

Found through much of the region except in the north-east.

Indian Peafowl   110 cms without train
Pavo cristatus   **Mor**

male

The Peafowl may be seen in the wild, walking elegantly through scrub or in deciduous forests. It is shy and can walk quickly enough to avoid humans but if disturbed, it will rise into the air revealing its wonderful 'tail' that is in reality an abnormally lengthened upper tail-covert; the female has no ornamental train and is of a more mottled appearance. This bird can be found close to human habitation being protected by religious sentiment. Feeds on grain, vegetable shoots, insects, lizards and snakes. Recognisable by its loud, echoing and penetrating call.

Found throughout the region.

female

Comb Duck
Sarkidiornis melanotos

76 cms
Nakta

male

Favours the *jheel* where there is both an abundance of vegetation as well as an open area of water. Can be sometimes seen perched on trees where it finds nest holes. A diver that also upends, might be seen walking over waterlogged fields to graze on grain and shoots, cultivated rice and vegetable matter. Not a vegeterian however, eats frogs and acquatic insects.

Resident but given to local movement within the region.

orange algae stains visible in front

Cotton Pygmy Goose (Cotton Teal)
Nettapus coromandelianus

33 cms
Girri Batakh

male in eclipse with an immature

Found on all inland waters such as *jheel*, ditches, paddyfields and tanks, it can be tamed if not harassed. Good at diving, it walks a little, feeding from the water surface. An agile flier, perching and nesting on the lower branches of trees.

Found through much of the region.

male

female

Lesser Whistling-duck
Dendrocygna javanica

42 cms
Choti Seethi

During the day, these birds often stand almost motionless, silently watching as animals do, preferring to feed at night and although largely vegetarian, they will eat snails and small fish. Often seen in groups that rest on vegetation growing over water, it sometimes dives and also perches on trees.

Widespread resident in the north and the west.

bird in flight showing its chestnut-coloured upper-tail coverts

Spot-billed Duck
Anas poecilorhyncha

58–63 cms
Gugral Battakh

While moving across the water, these ducks feed largely on what the surface of the water has to offer; they will also upend themselves. Often seen in isolated couples, the species are found throughout India, sometimes in numbers of up to fifty in one group but seldom more since they are residents and during the hot, much drier months, require water. They are considered to be good parents on account of the way they carefully guard their down-lined nests, built near water.

Widespread breeding resident.

Yellow-crowned Woodpecker
Dendrocopus mahrattensis

18 cms
Piltaj Kathfora

male

Inhabits open scub country with light deciduous forest, orchards and groves in proximity to villages. Can be seen moving quickly up tree-trunks, stopping every now and then before darting off again. Tapping and digging into rotting wood, in search of insects and grubs, it uses its tail as a rudder and support while clinging to the tree. The tongue is long and used to skewer grubs and draw them out from bores. Like other woodpeckers, its flight is swift and undulating — rapid wing-beats followed by gaps when the wings are withdrawn.

Absent in the north-east.

female

Black-rumped Flameback
Dinopium benghalense

Kalphuth Angara Kathfora

male

Found in areas where trees constitute a light jungle, particularly of mangoes, ancient tree-groves and coconut plantations. Slowly works its way up tree-trunks, along the boughs, winding its way, this way and that, reversing downwards, looking for food such as beetles and insects in nooks and crannies of the bark. Also eats food from the ground such as black ants as well as fruit pulp and flower nectar. The female is distinguished from the male by white streaks on the forecrown and a red hindcrown.

Widespread breeding resident.

female

9

Brown-headed Barbet
Megalaima zeylanica

27 cms
Kotur Basantha

This Barbet shares the characteristics of the Coppersmith Barbet (*see* opposite). Generally solitary but also congregating in groups when feeding on fruit trees. The diet may include figs, berries, insects as well as flowers and nectar. Often vocal during the breeding season with a monotonous call—'*kutroo*'.

Found in peninsular India and the north.

Coppersmith Barbet
Megalaima haemacephala

17 cms

Thathera Basantha

Although more subdued in winter, its name comes from the penetrating '*tok! tok!*' call that is similar to the sound of a coppersmith at work, a sound not often heard these days. The head pattern is a distinguishing characteristic. Eats winged insects caught during short sallies and also the fruit and berries from the banyan and *peepul* trees, roosting and nesting in holes excavated by both sexes in tree-trunks.

A widespread breeding resident.

One is more likely to hear than see the Grey Hornbill owing to its distinctive, electrifying cry. Found near human habitation, its natural habitat is medium forest. Flies with a few rapid flaps of the wing, gracefully dipping and rising as it moves along, its enormous beak pointing forward and the wing-tips upturned. Largely a frugivore, small rodents also constitute its diet.

A widespread breeding resident, largely absent in the east.

Common Hoopoe   31 cms
Upupa epops   **Hudhud**

The Hoopoe derives its name from its soft '*poop! poop! poop!*' cry and can be seen singly or in pairs, often around human habitation, sometimes digging the ground for food. Also eats insects and is thus popular among agriculturists. When alighting or surprised, reveals a fan-like crest.

Widespread as a breeding resident; a winter visitor to the west and summer visitor to the high Himalayas.

bird with crest revealed

13   BIRDS OF INDIA

Indian Roller
Coracias benghalensis

16–18 cms
Desi Neelkanth

The cyan colours of this bird make it very striking. Popular among agriculturists owing to its appetite for insects, it perches high in the open country from where it hunts for small rodents, battering its victim to death before eating. This bird displays a distinctive style of courtship.

A widespread breeding resident.

affinis

Little Green Bee-eater
Merops orientalis

From such a perch as the one seen here or from a more obvious one like a barbed wire fence, these birds will fly off to snap up a bee in their beaks, returning to kill and devour it. Where bees are unavailable, they make do with other insects. They are found in small, loose groups and inhabit a wide variety of habitats, ranging from open country to the coast.

A widespread breeding resident.

This is one of the most enjoyable birds to observe. From a vantage point above water, it watches the surface for signs of small fish moving, its head bobbing up and down every now and then or turning this way or that, to locate prey before diving into the water. Fishes usually in shallow, flowing water and can be seen flying low over the surface, making a shrill '*chiree-chiree*' sound as its bright-coloured body flashes past.

Inhabits streams to open waterbodies around the subcontinent.

Stork-billed Kingfisher 38 cms
Pelagopsis capensis **Barachonch Kilkila**

Inhabits well-watered country, keeping to shady streams, jungle pools, swampy glades and tidal creeks; in the east, it is more conspicuous being seen perched on telegraph wires, while elsewhere it tends to sit in the shade. Most easily identifiable when hurtling over water to find a suitable perch from where it scouts for prey; consumes crabs, fish, reptiles, frogs and occasionally young birds and eggs from nests. Either lets out a raucous '*ke-ke-ke-ke-ke!*' or a more relaxed '*peer-peer-pur!*'

Absent in the north-west.

White-throated Kingfisher   28 cms
Halycon smyrmensis   **Safed Choti Kilkila**

Usually perches on a slightly concealed branch to obtain a good view of water. About pigeon-sized, with a varied diet consisting of small amphibians, rodents, insects and smaller birds. Found not only near expanses of water but also on farmland where puddles form, providing suitable food. The call is a distinctive, loud '*chirrup*'.

Found throughout the region.

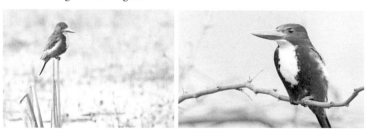

Pied Kingfisher   31 cms
Ceryle rudis   **Kaurilla Kilkila**

male to the left, female to the right

The male of this species is distinguished from the female by the unbroken band of black running across its chest; the female's is broken, revealing a fuller white chest. Can be spotted hovering several metres above water from where it might excitedly call before dropping, silently and swiftly, wings clasped to its sides, emerging with a tiny wriggling fish clasped firmly in its beak, if successful. Breeding is recorded all the year round.

A widespread breeding resident.

Pied Cuckoo
Clamator jacobinus

31 cms
Ablak Chatak

Lays its eggs in the nests of other birds for them to hatch and bring up. Keeps to the trees, although sometimes descends to ground level, hunting for food such as grasshoppers, caterpillars and occasionally berries.

A breeding resident in the south; summer visitor to the north and north-east.

Common Cuckoo
Cuculus canorus

33 cms
Kuphu Kuhuk

male

female

An insectivore that particularly likes hairy caterpillars and cicadas, the Common Cuckoo has a distinctive '*cuk-coo! cuk-coo!*' call; however, when breeding, it remains silent. Arboreal, showing preference for the canopy of well-wooded country. Parasitic, laying its eggs in the nests of smaller birds such as chats, pipits and buntings, forcing them to rear its young ones.

A breeding visitor and migrant found throughout most of the region.

hepatic

immature

Asian Koel
Eudynamys scolopacea

43 cms
Koel

male

While the male Koel is black in colour with a greenish gloss, the female has a spotted appearance with variegated feathers of white and brown. Often found concealed within trees and not easy to see, it emits a cry that is both raucous and piercing, heard most often during the breeding season. Can often be found near habitation, living on fruit and insect life. An arboreal fruit-eater also subsisting on insects and nectar.

A widespread breeding resident.

female

Sirkeer Malkoha
Taccocua leschenaultii

Lalmukhi Malkoha

A shy bird that tends to keep to cover, nesting in trees and building a saucer-shaped leaf-lined structure. By nature more of a terrestial bird, running with head and tail held horizontally. Consumes insects, lizards, fallen fruits and berries. In display, one bird circles the other, tail cocked, wings drooping.

Found in most of the Indian subcontinent but not in the north-east.

Greater Coucal
Centropus sinensis

48 cms
Barah Mahok

Also called Crow-Pheasant, it lets out a vibrant but low '*cou cou cou*' which can be heard resounding from the undergrowth. Particularly noisy during the breeding season when the male spreads out its wings and tail to dance in front of the female. The nest may be built in a bamboo thicket or high up a tree such as the tamarind. Subsists on a diet of insects, snails and small mammals; seen clambering awkwardly over vegetation.

Found in the north and along southern Indus valley; absent in the Himalayas.

juvenile

Southern Coucal
Centropus (sinensis) parroti

48 cms
Kooka

With a long bill but shorter legs and wings than the larger Greater Coucal. Breeds both in winter and spring rather than the monsoon when its call is slightly more high-pitched and less mellow. The dull, brownish forehead and throat are distinctive.

Found in central and the southern Indian peninsula.

Rose-ringed Parakeet
Psittacula krameri

42 cms
Samanya Tota

There are a number of different species of Parakeet in India of which the Rose Ringed is the most common. Has a shrill cry that can be heard not only when perching but also whilst flying. A nuisance to agriculture since it eats crops and orchard fruits, resulting in villagers killing the bird. Gregarious.

Found in most parts of the region; avoids dense forests.

Plum-headed Parakeet   37 cms
Psittacula cyanocephalia   **Twinya Tota**

male

Prefers wooded country. A very swift flyer, adroitly twisting and turning as it flies through woodland; maintains this movement when flying in a flock. While flying it gives out its distinctive call, a shrill '*tooi, tooi-tooi*'. Feeds on plant seeds and smaller fruits; nests in tree-holes.

Absent in the north-east and north-west.

female

BIRDS OF INDIA

House Swift   15 cms
Apus affinis   **Gharelu Ababeel Batasee**

As the name implies, this bird nests in houses, ruins such as old forts and deserted mosques. Also found amidst the bustle of modern cities. Flies at great speed when entering or leaving its nesting area. Visible when scouting for flies, midges or other small insects that constitute its diet; flies with mouth open wide as this helps in capturing prey. Peculiar claws on all the four toes point forward, preventing it from perching on a branch so that it can only hang from rough-textured ceilings and walls. A black plumage with a white rump is its distinctive characteristic.

Rarely seen in the north-east.

Spotted Owlet
Athene brama

21 cms
Samanya Khoosat

With silent staring eyes, this Owlet can be seen in trees and also among ruins, being more easily visible than other members of the owl family. Although hunting at night, it can be seen at dawn and dusk when its wheezy screech may be heard.

A widespread breeding resident.

Indian Scops-owl (Collared Scops-owl)   23 cms
Otus bakkamoena   **Galapatti Chugad**

The male Scops-owl seen here on the right, is smaller than the female, a characteristic known as sexual dimorphism. More easily heard rather than seen, it can be identified with its soft interrogative '*wut?*' call, audible at night. Hunts for food, mostly beetles and other insects, as well as mice and lizards.

Found over most of the region.

Brown Fish-owl
Ketupa zeylonensis

Apart from fish scooped near the surface of waterbodies, Fish-owls also eat a variety of frogs and crabs as well as rodents, reptiles and birds. Nests during the cooler season in the holes of trees as well as in the old nests of raptors.

Found over most of the region yet seldom seen in Pakistan.

Laughing Dove (Little Brown Dove)
Streptopelia senegalensis

27 cms
Chitrokha Fakhta

Likes dry, stony scrub country but is found near villages and cultivated areas too. Can be quite tame, roosting in the eaves of houses, eating seeds and grain picked from the ground, uttering a soft '*coo-rooroo-roorooo*'. The courtship pattern involves the male bobbing around on the ground. Executes stiff hops; while in display flight, has a silent arc-like descent. The male broods by day; the female at night.

Absent in the north-east.

Spotted Dove　　　　　　　　　　　　　　30 cms
Streptopelia chinensis　　　　　　　　　　　　**Tit Roon**

The Spotted Dove is seen on the ground in areas of habitation and cultivation. Perches on trees, avoiding areas that lack water. Nests at almost any time of the year, building a flimsy structure with just a few twigs at a very low height in a tree or bush. The call is soft yet slightly mournful, heard throughout the day.

A widespread breeding resident.

Red-collared Dove
Streptopelia tranquebarica

23 cms
Tent Kohari Fakhta

male

Red-collared Dove is found singly or in pairs, in open cultivated country. Feeds on grain and seeds from the ground. Emits a little harsh '*groo-gurr-goo, groo-gurr-goo*' call repeated quickly a few times. Nests the year round fairly high up on a tree or bush.

Found throughout the region; a summer visitor to Pakistan.

female on left (similar to the Eurasian Collared Dove)

Eurasian Collared Dove
Streptopelia decaocto

32 cms
Dharer Fakhta

Preferring dry country, particularly open and cultivated, this Dove likes groves where it can retire from the midday heat. Drawn to the neighbourhood of human habitation, often visiting gardens and verandahs. The call is a deep, trisyllabic '*kuk-koo-kook!*' repeated several times while the courtship pattern involves noisy flapping of the wings and fanning out of the tail in an aerial display.

Found in most parts of the region.

Rock Pigeon
Columba livia

33 cms
Samanya Kabutar

Often seen, Rock Pigeon is heard occasionally releasing a throaty '*gotoor-goo*' sound. One of only a few birds mentioned by the ancient scripture *Rig Veda*, it has become a familiar sight and sound around habitation. Interbreeding produces a feral stock; also inhabits wild places such as cliffs.

One of the most common birds of the region.

Yellow-footed Green Pigeon
Treron phoenicoptera

33 cms
Samanya Haryal

phoenicoptera

chlorigaster (green belly, grey tail)

The colours of this attractive bird that hardly ever comes to rest on the ground, makes it inconspicuous when roosting, often in flocks. The fig-bearing *peepul* and *banyan* trees are favourite haunts and it is quite acrobatic when moving around to pluck fruit from branches. The bird has a melodious whistle that moves up and down the scale. When disturbed, flight is straight and direct, accompanied by a loud flapping of wings. There are two recognised species, *Chlorigaster* and *Phoenicoptera*.

A widespread resident; of the two races, the *Phoenicopterus Phoenicoptera* is eastern.

Sarus Crane
Grus antigone

156 cms
Saras

male and female dancing

Also known as the Indian Crane, it mates for life. Reverence for the bird in India has helped it survive against the odds. The eastern form *sharpii* is called *Khur Sang* in Assam but has not been seen for nearly a century. A trumpeting call may be heard before its elegant form is seen. Observed in family groups as well as in pairs; flies with body outstretched, revealing a characteristic grace. Found in pairs, the family groups are not seen in large flocks.

A widespread resident.

unison call

White-breasted Waterhen   32 cms
Amaurornis phoenicurus   **Safed Chati Jal Murghi**

This species is seen during the day with its tail flicking up to reveal a patch of dull, red feathers behind as it wanders along. Normally silent but during the rainy season, when breeding, it becomes very noisy, emitting a '*wak wak wak!*' call. Has the habit of climbing on to the top of a bush to conceal itself. Nests on the ground in dense vegetation.

Found in most of the region.

Purple Swamphen
Porphyrio porphyrio

Jalmuni Jalmurgi

This Swamphen is very similar to the Waterhen in its characteristics though it is found in larger groups and prefers more watery habitats such as swampy ground. A vivid bluish-purple body makes it stand out from other birds and recognisable from a distance. The call is a mixture of hoarse-sounding notes with hoots and cackles. Walks over and eats vegetation that covers water.

A widespread resident.

Common Moorhen
Gallinula chloropus

32 cms
Samanya Jalmurgi

Found in pairs and groups, the Moorhen remains within partially submerged vegetation, swimming or skulking, often disappearing on one's approach. Swims more than the Whitebreasted Waterhen and flies low over water when necessary. Eats insects, worms, molluscs, grain and paddy shoots. Builds a bulky cup-nest above water.

Found over most of the Indian subcontinent.

Common Coot
Fulica atra

42 cms
Tikdi

This resident, whose limited numbers get a boost during the winter months, particularly in the north by immigrants from central and western Asia, can be seen in large groups on water. Takes off by skittering along the water's surface somewhere between running and flying before rising into the air; once aloft, the bird is a strong flyer. The flight is distinguished from that of a duck by hovering wing beats, blunt barrel-shaped body and trailing legs. Feeds on vegetation, insects and molluscs.

Found throughout the region.

Black-tailed Godwit
Limosa limosa

46 cms
Bara Gudera

western non-breeding (limosa)

At low tide, this Godwit is seen 'hunting' along the water's edge, probing into the soft mud with a long bill in search of molluscs, worms, crabs and insects. Seen in flocks with other waders, frequenting both fresh and brackish-water habitats. Often wades into deeper water, submerging its head while looking for food.

A winter visitor to western India.

eastern in flight (melanuroides)

Pintail Snipe
Gallinago stenura

Seen singly or in small numbers except at the begining or end of migration, probing the mud for food usually at dawn or dusk or during the night. While resting during the day, its colours provide excellent camouflage. The diet consists largely of larvae, worms and molluscs. Flies lower than Common Snipe.

A winter visitor to most of the region.

Common Snipe   26 cms
Gallinage gallinago   **Samanya Chaha**

Common Snipe favours wet areas of ground as well as the grassy edges of
jheels (lakes) and salt-water estuaries though it may wade in shallow waters.
A master of disguise, blending into the background even when out in the
open. If disturbed, the bird will fly out suddenly, uttering a rather harsh cry
to dissappear in a fast zig-zag flight. The diet consists of worms, insect life
and such food that it finds in soft mud when probing with the long, slender
beak. A skulker, also feeding at night.

Although a winter migrant, the Snipe spends September to April in India.
Found in most of the region.

Common Redshank
Tringa totanus

28 cms
Chota Soorma Chaubaha

beginning breeding

This Redshank shares characteristics with the Sandpipers with whom it is often seen. Red legs are a distinctive characteristic as are the buff bars on the white tail. The breeding colours are marked by heavier streaks. Usually solitary, it feeds by running around, picking up morsels found alongside *jheels* and estuaries.

A winter migrant to much of India; breeds in the far north of India and Pakistan.

non-breeding

Common Greenshank
Tringa nebularia

36 cms
Bara Timtima Chaubaha

Often solitary, sometimes in small groups, the Greenshank may be found in the company of the Redshank. The bill is slightly upturned. A wader, one chief characteristic of this bird is the way it runs in a straight line with its bill underwater and neck outstretched. The diet comprises tadpoles and frogs, insects and other invertebrates while its call is a '*teu! teu! teu!*' which is often uttered in flight or when disturbed.

A widespread winter visitor.

Green Sandpiper
Tringa ochropus

21–24 cms
Hara Chaubaha

summer

Of somewhat stocky build, Green Sandpiper has light green legs. Rather a shy bird that will take off on being approached, it likes to forage where other waders are not present, particularly in pools. Finds food either in mud or water amidst the marginal vegetation growing in the shallows of marshes and creeks.

A widespread winter visitor.

winter

Wood Sandpiper
Tringa glareola

21 cms
Bhoora Chaubaha

breeding

A common and gregarious bird, found near inland waters and in marshes, flooded paddyfields and tidal mudflats. A wader, walks over mudflats to search for tit-bits probing (with its bill) into the mud. The tail may bob up and down in an exaggerated fashion. The diet consists of insects, larvae, worms and molluscs. Favours more of an open habitat.

A winter visitor to most of the region; a summer breeder in the north.

non-breeding

Common Sandpiper
Tringa hypoleucos

21 cms
Samanya Chaubaha

This wader spends most of the year in the region, breeding in the far north. Not a bird seen in flocks, unless circumstances dictate, it inhabits ponds, tanks, tidal creeks as well as rocky seashores. The diet is like that of other Sandpipers.

Found throughout the region.

Eurasian Thick-knee (Indian Stone-curlew)
Burhinus indicus

41 cms
Ureshiyan Kavarn

A bird of dry plains and scanty scrub, ploughed fields, dried river-beds and light jungle, it is often found close to human habitation. Can be seen during the day standing motionless being a largely crepuscular and nocturnal bird. If disturbed during the day, it will squat on the ground with neck extended. Easily camouflaged against probing eyes due to colouration. Lives on a diet of insects, worms and small reptiles, adding grit to them to aid in digestion. Gregarious.

Found in most of the region; not so common in Pakistan and the north-east.

nests on ground in hollow scrape

Little Stint
Calidris minuta

13 cms
Chota Panalwa

A gregarious and sociable bird, this Stint is often found in a group of other wader species. Inhabiting marshes and tidal mudflats, the flock will spread out as they feed, running over the mud in search of tiny insects, crustaceans and molluscs. If disturbed, the birds fly off immediately in a tightly orchestrated flock, twisting and turning on their way. Black legs are a distinctive characteristic.

A winter visitor found particularly along the coasts.

Temminick's Stint
Calidris temminckii

14 cms
Temminick Panalwa

breeding

Not gregarious, this Stint is also found among groups of other waders. Has similar characteristics to the Little Stint yet feeds more slowly, often amidst vegetation. If disturbed, the bird flies straight upwards with a rather erratic flight. White sides to the tail are a major distinctive feature.

A winter visitor to the north of the region.

non-breeding

Pheasant-tailed Jacana
Hydrophasianus chirurgus

31 cms
Peeho

non-breeding adult

A bird with similar characteristics to those of the Bronze-winged Jacana, having the same spidery, elongated toes. During the breeding season, the tail curves and becomes much longer, typically as long as the bird itself. Feeds on vegetable matter, aquatic insects and molluscs. Often found in flocks of 50 or so, feeding on prey caught near the surface of the water.

Throughout the region; a summer visitor to northern Pakistan.

immature

Bronze-winged Jacana   28–31 cms
Metopidius indicus   **Peepee**

adult

Once the adroit claws develop fully, Jacana can be seen walking across the surface of a well-covered pond or lake, using its elongated and spreading toes to do so. Can swim well and occasionally dives partially submerging itself when alarmed. Builds a sheltered nest amidst vegetation.

A widespread resident.

claw

immature

Black-winged Stilt
Himantopus himantopus

35–40 cms
Gaj Paon

immature

This Stilt hunts for food in shallow waters, working backwards and forwards in an area when probing in mud for worms, molluscs and aquatic insects. At times it submerges its head and neck beneath the surface of water. Often feeds in small groups that include other waders. A graceful walker with exaggerated steps, even with water up to its belly, it can swim though not very skilfully.

A widespread resident.

adult

Little-ringed Plover
Charadrius dubius

17 cms
Jeera Batan

non-breeding

A bird that frequents mudflats, shingle banks and the sandy pits of rivers, as well as inland waters and lakes. Often seen in small parties. Has the curious habit of runnning in short spurts before stopping again in search of food. The colouration helps it to merge into the background although quick movements give it away. While feeding, the group spreads out but when disturbed, the whole group will fly away emitting a short plaintive call; the flight pattern is a twisting one.

Found throughout the region.

breeding

BIRDS OF INDIA

Red-wattled Lapwing
Vanellus indicus

This Lapwing has a piercing cry sometimes alliterated as '*Did he do it? Pity to do it!*' Visible on open grazing land, the borders of ponds and by puddles, also spotted in forest clearings. Characteristically, runs about then stops, dipping forward to pick up food in the form of insects, molluscs as well as grubs. Forms groups yet pairs more common during the breeding season.

A widespread resident.

Often found in flocks on bare stony ground or waste and fallow land near cultivation, this Courser feeds on beetles and their larvae, crickets and grasshoppers among other insects. Moves around in a zig-zag fashion, dipping forward every now and then. If disturbed, runs forward a few yards before stopping suddenly to stand erect and survey the intruder; when threatened, utters a hoarse '*gwaat*' call before flying off low over the ground, landing and then running further.

Found in the drier regions but not in the east.

Ruff
Philomachus pugnax

Gregarious and often found with other waders with whom it shares some basic characteristics, Ruff like to eat seeds from weed. They look most impressive during the breeding season when the males develop ruffs, striking feathery collars. Courtship displays can be confrontational. More often seen during the winter months, sometimes wading into deep water and swimming.

Found mostly in the west of the region.

near breeding

Small Pratincole
Glareola lactea

17 cms
Choti Ghobaucha

Somewhat crepuscular, the Pratincole hunts deep into the night. Flocks tend to be scattered and hawk insects from the air. Runs in short spurts, stopping when food is found. Feeds on insects caught in mid-air often close to the water's surface. Sometimes called Swallow-plover as it resembles swallows in flight.

A resident to much of the region; a summer visitor to the north-west.

Black-headed Gull
Larus ridibundus

38 cms
Kalsheersh Dhomra

Found along the sea-coast, in estuaries and harbours, this Gull forms flocks. Can be seen scavenging in garbage and also for scraps thrown from boats which it trails. Scoops food from the water's surface, yet also seen floating. The diet further includes insects, grubs and slugs as well as the shoots of crops. Closely related to the slightly larger Brown-headed Gull (42 cms). The head turns black during breeding.

Found along the coasts of the region and inland too.

River Tern
Sterna aurantia

42 cms
Jal Kurrri

adult

Flies with continued wingbeats, a few metres or so above water, scanning the surface for fish; when striking, it closes its wings and dives steeply. The prey is clasped sideways across the bill and when flying again, the prey is swallowed head first. Apart from fish, it also eats crustaceans as well as tadpoles and insect life. Often seen in small groups, flying about 8 or 10 metres above the water surface and into the wind with a rather jerky flight. Breeds during the summer in Pakistan while in India, breeding is from November onwards. Sandbars and islands found in major rivers provide potential spots for nesting.

Found throughout the region.

juvenile

Oriental Honey-buzzard
Pernis ptilorhynchus

A bird of the forest and more open woodland, the Buzzard feeds on the honey and larvae of wild bees as well as wasps although its diet commonly consists of insects, small mammals, lizards and small birds. Tends to be a rather silent bird except during the breeding season. Nests on a platform of sticks.

Found throughout the region.

Black-shouldered Kite (Black-winged Kite)
Elanus caeruleus

33 cms
Kapassi Cheel

This Kite can be seen hovering above grassland before dropping to the ground in a parachute-like motion, grabbing its prey in a pair of claws — the prey may be a locust, a cricket, a mouse, a lizard or some such creature. The Kite prefers the night to the day for hunting and likes a locality where it can find an appropriate place to perch. Prefers open and drier lowland, feeding mostly on mammals but also on reptiles and insects. Builds a twig nest.

A widespread resident.

65

BIRDS OF INDIA

Black Kite (Pariah Kite)
Milvus migrans

This most common and easily seen bird of prey habituates towns and cities. Often seen circling in the sky overhead, adroitly turning on the wing. Nests on buildings as well as in trees and lets out a raucous musical whistle. Feeds on vermin and can be seen in dozens above or near garbage dumps. There are different races of this species with varying kinds of morph.

Commonly found as a resident and winter visitor.

Brahminy Kite
Haliastur indus

48 cms
Safed-sir Cheel

Found in the vicinity of villages and harbours where it scavenges for scraps and garbage; also frequents rivers, *jheel* and inundated paddy fields, moving inland during the monsoon season to feed on land crabs and frogs. Otherwise, the diet is offal, small snakes, bats and insects such as winged termites that it waits for as they emerge from sodden ground. The call is a hoarse and wheezy whistle.

A breeding resident found throughout the region.

Egyptian Vulture
Neophron percnopterus

64 cms
Safed gidh

A scavenger, found in open country and in the neighbourhood of human habitation; can be seen walking over the ground with a characteristic waddling gait or 'goose step'. Much of the diet comes from offal and human excrement, also feeding off animal carcasses. An interesting behaviour trait is an ability to kill and consume stranded fresh-water turtles. A communal rooster.

Found through much of the region but not in the north-east.

Red-headed Vulture　　　　　　　　　　　　84 cms
Sarcogyps calvus　　　　　　　　　　　　**Raj Gidh**

Although also known as King Vulture, this vulture is actually more timid than others when seen in a group thronging around carrion. Eats other food such as large insects, frogs, reptiles as well as the eggs and young of birds. Usually seen alone or in pairs, stealing food from other birds.

Found throughout the region, particularly in the central north.

White-bellied Sea Eagle
Haliaeetus leucogaster

A bird of the coastline and estuary, the Sea Eagle earmarks territories that can be occupied by a single pair for many years unless disturbed. Feeds on fish and sea-snakes, catching its prey in talons when the victim swims near the surface of the water; does not dive into the water. Soars. Nests during the winter months, high in a tree. The nest is made of large twigs often lined with green leaves; such nests are used year after year being repaired with new sticks when necessary.

Found all along the Indian coastline, except in the west and in Pakistan.

Crested Serpent Eagle
Spilornis cheela

56–74 cms
Dogra Cheel

This eagle likes to sit on a sheltered branch providing a commanding view of the surrounding countryside. Can also be seen flying over forested areas in both the hills and plains where there is a good supply of water. The diet does not consist merely of snakes as its name implies, often eating frogs, lizards and rats. Sometimes heard rather than seen, it can be identified by call of '*klee-klee-kleeuw*!'

A widespread resident, absent in large parts of the west.

Shikra
Accipiter badius

36 cms
Shikra (male) **Cheepak** (female)

A bird of prey that likes to occupy a high vantage point such as a leafy branch from where it can swoop down and catch its prey unawares. Avoids heavy forest, preferring more open wooded country, often the groves of large trees near habitation. Flies close to the ground with rapid wing-beats also gliding. The diet consists of smaller birds as well as squirrels, mice, lizards and so forth.

A widespread breeding resident, not found in the high Himalayas.

male

Steppe Eagle
Aquila nipalensis

Roosting and migrating communally, the Steppe Eagle perches on high branches from where it can pounce on prey that could be a small mammal, bird, reptile, or insect. Steals food from smaller birds of prey, also hunting from the ground, waiting for mammals to catch. Prefers a habitat of wooded hills, large lakes and open country. A yellow gape extends to the back of the eye in this bird.

A widespread winter visitor.

BIRDS OF INDIA

Common Kestrel
Falco tinnunculus

36 cms
Samanya Kheramutiya

The Kestrel is a bird of prey that hovers above the ground for extended periods before plummeting downwards to grasp a small mammalian prey in its claws. Has the ability to see a different colour spectrum that highlights the urine of its prey and so helps in locating it. Builds a nest in an old building, cliff or disused raptor nest.

A winter visitor and breeding resident in the west of Indian peninsula and also Pakistan.

Little Grebe   25–29 cms
Tachybaptus ruficollis   **Chota Dubdubi**

breeding plumage

Also known as 'Dabchick', this small water-bird may be seen on inland waters throughout most of India. Swims well and is an excellent diver that can disappear almost without trace. Although tending to keep to the water, it can fly well when circumstances dictate. Lives on aquatic life varying from insect-sized prey to frogs.

Found throughout the region at all times of the year.

non-breeding plumage

Darter (Snake Bird)
Anhinga melanogaster

90 cms
Baanvai

The Darter can be seen perched atop branches near open water while drying its wings in the sun being a bird that can swim under water. The head is thin, neck elongated, and it can be seen gliding above, before it dives below to catch the fish that constitutes its diet. Occasionally, spearing the fish or killing it with a blow delivered with a quick jab of the bill. Nests in colonies.

A widespread breeding resident.

Little Cormorant
Phalacrocorax niger

51 cms

Chota Pan Kowwa

breeding plumage

Sometimes found in groups, the Little Cormorant hunts in groups, living on fish. Found in fresh as well as sea-water areas; can be seen perched near water, on rocks or even high up on trees. Like the Darter, catches fish by diving into the water and swimming underneath the surface to catch prey.

A breeding resident throughout the Indian subcontinent, not found in the Himalayas or far west.

juvenile

Indian Cormorant (Indian Shag)
Phalacrocorax fuscicollis

63 cms
Desi Pan Kowwa

non-breeding

Although less ubiquitous than the other two Cormorants, this bird is gregarious and is found in their company even when fishing. Prefers a diet that contains exclusively fish. Inhabits small lakes and rivers, nesting in mixed colonies during the monsoon season.

Found throughout the region, except in the Himalayas and western Pakistan.

breeding

Great Cormorant
Phalacrocorax carbo

breeding plumage

Although sharing similar habitats and behavioural characteristics with other Cormorants, this species prefers to be alone when feeding. Dives and swims partially submerged, breeding in large twig nests during late monsoon.

Found in the Indian subcontinent.

Grey Heron
Ardea cinerea

Although often seen during the day, the Grey Heron tends to be more active at dawn and dusk. Stands hunched up, waiting for prey or stealthily wading through shallower water, looking intently for prey and seizing it quickly.

Found widespread as a breeding resident and winter visitor.

Purple Heron
Ardea purpurea

juvenile

The Purple Heron is not so easily seen as the other herons, preferring to hunt for prey in more secluded areas. Croaks and flies off if disturbed. Crepuscular by nature.

A widespread breeding resident not seen in the far north.

Little Egret
Egretta garzetta

55–65 cms
Karchia Bagla

It is easier to tell the Egrets apart during the breeding season when the colours are more pronounced. The Little Egret has a black beak and legs with yellow feet. Seen in groups that prefer areas where there is enough surface water to provide a meal of insects, fish, frogs and small reptiles. May retire to a perch to eat.

A widespread breeding resident.

Great Egret
Casmerodius albus

65–72 cms
Malang Bagla

full breeding plumage

A more solitary bird than others of the Egret family, the Great lives and hunts in deeper waters. Favouring a similar habitat to that of the Grey Heron, it feeds on fish, frogs and such creatures. A crick in the neck is a distinctive feature as is the gape extending behind the eye.

A widespread resident and occasional winter visitor absent in far north.

non-breeding

83

Intermediate Egret
Mesophoyx intermedia

65–72 cms
Patokha Bagla

Like other Egrets, this bird feeds on frogs and such creatures, first battering prey senseless before devouring it. The feathery aigrette in this species hangs only from the front and back, distinguishing it from others who also sport a delicate tuft of hair hanging from their neck that was once much sought after by milliners. Intermediate Egrets make stick nests in mixed colonies and hunt with an erect posture.

A widespread breeding resident.

Cattle Egret
Bubulcus ibis

48–53 cms
Gai Bagla

The Cattle Egret is so called because of a habit of following cattle and perching on their backs to obtain a good view of surroundings as the forms of life on which it feeds get disturbed. A common sight is to see this Egret walk around the slow-moving grazing cattle. The plumage is largely white but changes during the breeding season. Two sub-species of Cattle Egret exist — Western and Eastern.

A widespread breeding resident.

Indian Pond Heron
Ardeola grayii

non-breeding

This rather extraordinary looking bird is found almost anywhere near water, be it a village pond, a stream, a river or even the seashore. Can stand for hours, hunched up, waiting for movement from edible sources like frogs, fish, crabs and insects. Every now and then walks in search of prey. In flight, muted mottled colours give way to the white of its wings. Emits a harsh croak when flushed. Builds nests in bushes and trees.

Found throughout the region at heights up to 1,000 metres.

breeding

A bird that prefers marshy land which it walks across in search of food, using a peculiarly shaped bill like a pair of forceps to probe into the soft mud. This Ibis feeds in small groups often in the company of other birds. Nests during the monsoon.

A widespread breeding resident.

juvenile

Black-crowned Night Heron
Nycticorax nycticorax

58–65 cms
Waak Bagla

adult

During the day, small colonies of this bird gather in oft-frequented roosts and only really come to life during the night. Can be seen at dusk, flying out to hunting grounds to eat crabs, fish, frogs, aquatic insects and the like, fishing in the same distinctive manner as other herons. The call is a '*weck*' or '*kwock*' made when flying.

A widespread breeding resident.

juvenile

Indian Black Ibis
Pseudibis papillosa

73 cms
Kala Bujja

Usually found at a distance from water, this bird has its favourite locations and likes to roost on trees. Often seen in drier areas feeding on insects, grain and reptiles. The call is a loud, nasal scream, uttered when flying.

Found throughout India; a summer visitor to Pakistan; absent in the Himalayas and the north-east.

Eurasian Spoonbill
Platalea leucorodia

80–90 cms
Chamcha

The Spoonbill frequents marshes, ponds and mud-banks around areas of inland water. The long spatulate bill plays an important role in feeding as the lower part of the beak is used to rake up the mud under the water to search out tadpoles and molluscs, frogs, insects and vegetable matter. By methodically hunting in flocks across an area, their success rate increases by an estimated 80–90 per cent.

A resident, winter visitor in west and north.

Spot-billed Pelican
Pelicanus philippensis

152 cms
Chittichaunch Hawasil

One of three Pelicans found in the region, Spot-billed Pelicans live in large groups. They hunt communally, driving the fish into shallower waters by splashing their wings until the fish is scooped up in the huge pouch-like beak. Although the bird is large, it takes off almost effortlessly and can be seen flying around in circles at great heights. Lives in stick-nest colonies (often with Storks) from October to May.

A breeding resident found sporadically throughout the subcontinent.

BIRDS OF INDIA

Painted Stork
Mycteria leucocephala

93–100 cms
Jangdhil

The Painted Stork spends a lot of time standing with hunched up shoulders. Hunts by sauntering across grassy marshland, the swaying beak partially immersed in the shallow waters while searching for fish, frogs or snakes.

A widespread breeding resident.

Asian Openbill   68 cms
Anastomus oscitans   **Ghonghil**

adult

Openbill is a common Stork characterised by an open crack or gap in the bill. The diet includes frogs, crabs, large insects and other smaller forms of life. Breeds in human-disturbed areas.

A widespread breeding resident, not seen in the far north.

chick

The Woolly-necked Stork likes well-watered flat areas where the presence of water helps support food such as fish, frogs, reptiles, crabs, molluscs and large insects. Walks around and also flies, soaring aloft and circling. By nature rather shy and solitary.

A breeding resident, it sometimes migrates.

Black-necked Stork
Ephippiorhynchus asiaticus

135 cms
Loharangjal

female

After the breeding season, the adult and the young Storks can be seen moving in parties, though generally this bird is seen alone or in pairs. Has recognised feeding territories like large marshes, *jheel* and rivers. Wades in shallow water in search of fish, frogs, reptiles, crabs and other small creatures. Can occasionally be observed squatting on dry land while during the hotter part of the day, it may circle and soar in the sky above.

A breeding resident found sporadically throughout the region.

BIRDS OF INDIA

Bay-backed Shrike
Lanius vittatus

18 cms
Matiya Lahtora

Inhabits semi-desert areas avoiding pure desert and humid forests; likes drier areas of cultivation abounding in thorny scrub and waste land. Perches low on exposed bush-tops from where it swoops down to catch locusts, lizards, mice and such creatures.

Found through most of the region, a summer visitor to the far north-west.

Long-tailed Shrike
Lanius schach

erythronotus

Likes patches of thorny scrub and waste land hunting from an exposed perch before swooping down to carry off locusts, lizards, mice and similar creatures. Prey after being caught may be impaled on a thorn as is the custom with other Shrikes. The call is harsh yet when breeding sings a pleasant song.

Found throughout the region, a winter visitor in the south-east and a summer visitor in the north.

caniceps

tricolour

Southern Grey Shrike
Lanius meridionalis

25 cms
Dakshni Sileti Lahtora

lahtora

aucheri

There are three different species of this Shrike — *pallidirostris*, *lahtora* and *aucheri*. Like other Shrikes, this bird favours a place from which it can swoop down on prey such as a locust, lizard or mouse that is held underfoot before being ripped apart with the hooked bill and eaten. The victim is sometimes impaled on a thorn or other sharp object, a characteristic of Shrikes.

Found through much of the region; absent in the deep south and central parts of the east.

Rufous Treepie
Dendrocitta vagabunda

46–50 cms
Lal Tarupik

Found in wooded country and scrub jungle, this Treepie enters even inhabited areas and can be an extremely noisy visitor possessing a number of calls — some pleasant, others guttural. Essentially omnivorous, eating fruits, insects, lizards, frogs, centipedes, carrion and raiding the nests of other birds for both their eggs and chicks. Treepie nests are usually well concealed with the parental duties being jointly shared by the male and female of the species.

A widespread breeding resident absent in the far north.

House Crow
Corvus splendens

A very common bird in villages, towns and cities, the House Crow lives in close association with man. Audacious and cunning, it will eat almost anything from carrion to insects, fruit and grain, even the eggs and fledglings of other birds. A scavenger.

Found throughout the region.

Large-billed Crow (Jungle Crow)
Corvus macrorhynchos culminatus

49 cms
Lumb-chonch Kauwa

As the name implies, this bird does not live very close to man being more of a bird of the countryside. Omnivorous, eating smaller birds as well as young mammals.

A breeding resident throughout the region; not so commonly seen in Pakistan.

male

A bird that keeps to the trees and frequents countryside that is well-wooded yet open. Can often be found in groves of large trees close to habitation, as well as in gardens and on the sides of busy, noisy roads. The flight is strong yet dipping. Eats insects, figs as well as other fruits, berries and the nectar of flowers.

Found through most of the region; a winter visitor in south and summer visitor in north.

juvenile (playing with a feather)

Black-headed Oriole   25 cms
Oriolus xanthornus   **Topidar Peelak**

The behaviour of this bird is very similar to that of Eurasian Golden Oriole but with a less harsh and rather fluid call interspersed with guttural sounds such as a harsh '*kwark*' or noises similar to those of Treepies. Arboreal.

Found in much of the region but not in the north-west.

juvenile

Small Minivet   15 cms
Pericrocotus cinnamomeus   **Chota Rajalal**

male

A bird of the trees, this Minivet is found in light deciduous forest though it may visit gardens and groves. Flocks of the bird are larger in winter when these birds do not breed and the sexes segregate. Flits around the tree-tops eating insects and larvae.

Found through most of the region.

female

Found in pairs that keep to a restricted locality yet hunt with other groups of smaller birds that are likewise insectivores. From tree to tree, from twig to twig, this Fantail seems indefatigable as it waltzes and pirouettes, making graceful sallies after flies and even looping-the-loop if necessary. The call is a harsh '*chuck-chuck!*' yet its song is much sweeter, rendered as '*chee-chee-cheweechee-vi !*' uttered as it prances around.

Found over most of the region but not in the far north.

Black Drongo
Dicrurus macrocercus

31 cms
Samanya Bhujanga

A familiar bird recognisable by the white spot near its beak, Black Drongo can often be seen perched on telegraph wires and other points of vantage from where it swoops down to catch insects particularly grasshoppers. Sometimes rides atop the backs of cattle which disturb edible insects; will even approach forest fires to find insects on the move. Agriculturists are fond of this voracious, pest-eating bird.

Found through most of the region; a summer visitor in the far north.

Asian Paradise Flycatcher
Terpsiphone paradisi

20–50 cms

Safed Nar

The adult male Asian Paradise Flycatcher is one of India's most striking birds with its long, white tail that flaps behind the bird as it flies through the canopy of open forests, groves, bamboos, jungle scrubs and gardens. The female is not so flamboyant and tends to be found below the canopy. There is another race where the male is rufous on the back and the tail.

A breeding resident in the south, yet some migrate north during the hotter months.

Common Iora 14 cms
Aegithina tiphia **Samanya Shovigi**

male

A bird of the trees, found in town gardens, groves of trees on the outskirts of towns, as well as secondary jungle. Common Iora can be seen hopping around from twig to twig even hanging upside down as it acrobatically searches for insects, their eggs and larvae. It communicates through its musical whistle and a short '*chirrup*'. When courting, the male springs up into the air, fluffing out his feathers while uttering a variety of whistles before spiralling back to his perch.

A breeding resident through most of the region; absent in the north-west.

female

Inhabits scrubland and bush country as well as deciduous forest. Can be seen in gardens, roadside trees and the groves of trees such as the *neem* and *babul* as well as cultivated areas in the vicinity of villages. Hunts in parties often in the company of other birds. The diet consists largely of moths, beetles, caterpillars and similar creatures that are found on trees and occasionally in the air. Not very shy.

Found through most of the region.

Blue Rock-Thrush
Monticola solitarius

23 cms
Kasmiri Sail Kastura

male

male

A solitary bird, bolder when not breeding, this Rock-thrush frequents rocky boulder-strewn hillsides, rock scarps, ruins and inhabited buildings. Likes to perch on top of a prominent rock and when agitated, displays a series of exaggerated postures, tipping forward until its breast almost touches the ground before again standing erect. Keeps to a certain neighbourhood, returning after migration. Although a berry eater, it is largely an insectivore, flying from its perch in a sally close to the ground, eating prey immediately. In case the insect is too large, the creature is brought back to the perch, knocked senseless and then swallowed.

Visitor from October to April in most parts of the region; a summer visitor in the north.

female

Grey-headed Canary Flycatcher
Culicicapa ceylonensis

Pilapeti Machariya

A bird that seeks shelter under a canopy from where it makes aerial flycatching sallies, typical of other Flycatchers. Noisy and conspicious, being active and acrobatic in its search for food. The call is a twittering high-pitched '*chik-whichee-whichee*'. Nests from April to June, building a mossy cobweb-bound cup in a tree or on a rock.

A breeding resident in some areas, more commonly seen during the winter.

Bluethroat
Luscinia svecica

15 cms
Neelkanthi Loo Seeniya

male

female

Likes the water's edge amidst reeds and bushes where it hunts for insect life, hopping and stopping every now and then till it comes across suitable prey which can include caterpillars and tiny beetles. Seen characteristically with tail cocked and head drooping. The bird is categorised into three races, differentiated by red and white-marking on the throat.

Found throughout much of India during the winter months; during summer, breeds in the western Himalayas.

Oriental Magpie Robin   23 cms
Copsychus saularis   **Dhayal**

male

Familiarly seen around towns and villages, this Robin keeps to the shrubbery, yet becomes more vocal during the breeding season when the male can be heard singing sweetly from a vantage point, jerking its tail every now and then. A territorial bird that challenges intruding males, nesting in the hole of a tree or wall, fairly close to the ground. Lives mainly on insects and nectar, yet has been known to take Gecko as prey. Confiding, forages on the ground.

A widespread breeding resident, but not in the far north.

female

Indian Robin   19 cms
Saxicoloides fulicata   **Kalchuree**

male

The adult male Robin, seen here in a typically territorial pose, is another of the more common birds around human habitation and largely fearless of man. Likes stony scrub country, yet also visible on the rooves of huts and near houses, searching for insects that include spiders as well as insect eggs. Hops in a bouncing motion over the ground with the tail pointed upward, revealing a reddish vent.

Found through most of the region, but not in the north-east.

juvenile

female

Black Redstart 15 cms
Phoenicurus ochruros **Kala Thirthira**

male

Seen in the vicinity of villages and cultivated areas and amidst groves of trees, dry scub jungle as well as on ground-level hummocks. The bird flits around from perch to perch with a quivering tail. Lives off insects, particularly spiders usually taken from the ground although it can catch winged insects when flying.

A winter visitor to much of the region; a summer visitor to the far north.

female

Common Stonechat   13 cms
Saxicola torquata; maura (above) and *przewalski* (below) **Samanya Bhat Pidda**

non-breeding male

breeding male

The Common Stonechat frequents open country, fallow land, reedy margins of tanks, marshes as well as coastal areas. Feeds on insects and watches its prey from a reed stem or bush-top, flicking its tail up and down. The call is a '*chek! chek!*'. Often found in pairs.

A winter visitor to north and central India; Himalayan resident and summer visitor to Pakistan.

breeding female

breeding male

Pied Bushchat   13 cms
Saxicola caprata   **Ablak Jhara Pidda**

female (with tongue out)

The Pied Bushchat likes to perch on the top of a tree stump, reed or bush for making sallies after insects. This bird will also fly upwards to catch its prey. During the breeding season, sings not just to attract the female but also to keep off rival males while simultaneously revealing body movements that include drooping of the wings and showing off of the fluffy white backside. Likes deforested, agricultural areas.

Found through most of the region.

male

first-year male

Chestnut-tailed Starling (Grey-headed Myna)   21 cms
Sturnia malabarica   **Pavi Maina**

Arboreal by nature, this bird is seen in noisy flocks amidst thinly forested country, both close and far away from human habitation. The flight is swift and direct with a diet composed of insects as well as berries, figs and flower-nectar. The bird is a squabbler, chattering incessantly yet uttering few pleasant notes. Nests in an old tree-hole that it lines with twigs, rootlets and grass. Domestic duties are shared by the couple.

A breeding resident in the east; winter visitor to peninsular India; a summer visitor and migrant to the north.

Brahminy Starling (Brahminy Myna)   22 cms
Sturnus pagodarum   **Puhaya**

This bird likes moist grassland as well as open and well-cultivated areas. Perches on moving cattle that disturb the insects it feeds on, though it will eat almost anything edible, particularly wild fruits. Often frequents and yet is indifferent to human habitation.

A breeding resident in most of the region.

Asian Pied Starling (Pied Myna)   23 cms
Sturnus contra   **Abalkee Maina**

The Pied Myna makes noisy, communal roosts and can be seen circling around the area in large flocks. Feeds largely on the ground, digging, yet also eating grain, ripe fruit and flower-matter. Their inconspicuous nests are not built high.

A widespread resident in the north and east.

Common Myna   23 cms
Acridotheres tristis   **Desi Maina**

Found close to human habitation, this omnivorous bird likes to eat fruit, insects and left-overs discarded from kitchens. Seen around cultivators who work in the fields as well as following cattle for the edible life they disturb. Has a loud call.

Commonly found throughout the region.

Found in well-wooded localities but not in the denser, humid forests, hunts for insects with other birds, eating their eggs and larvae; also eats the buds of flowers and fruits. Using their feet to clasp the kernels of small nuts and seeds, the strong conical bill is used to break them open. The call during the breeding season is a loud and cheery whistle '*whee-chichi, whee-chichi, whee-chichi*'.

Found through most of the region but not along the eastern coast of India.

Barn Swallow (Common Swallow)   18 cms
Hirundo rustica   **Samanya Ababeel**

The Barn Swallow can be seen swooping and curling in flight as it hawks for winged insects either high up in the air or close to the ground, including the surface of water. A few wingbeats are followed by a glide, an overall swift and graceful movement; the forked tail plays an important role in these agile acrobatics directed towards capturing flies and midges. The nest is a half-cup of mud and vegetation stuck to the underside of buildings such as a shop or a bridge.

A winter visitor to much of the continent; a summer visitor to the Himalayas.

tytleri

123   BIRDS OF INDIA

Red-whiskered Bulbul   20 cms
Pyconotus jocosus   **Sipahi Bulbul**

Although this bird shares many characteristics with other Bulbuls, it is often found in more wooded localities, tending to prefer habitats different to the Red-vented Bulbul. It can be tame and confiding, entering gardens. The call is somewhat more musical and can be readily distinguished from that of the Red-vented Bulbul although the notes of both these birds are joyous and querulous.

Found throughout the region but not in the north-west.

Red-vented Bulbul
Pycnonotus cafer

A bird seen around the garden as well as scrub jungle, the Bulbul has no good singing voice though it makes cheerful enough noises being something of a favourite among the birds that frequent human habitation and seen in large swarms on *peepul* and *banyan* trees, eating the fruit but also has a varied diet consisting of insects, vegetables and flower-nectar. Sometimes kept as a pet, it has been used for fighting. Loose flocks are seen in the open.

A widespread breeding resident.

Eastern race (benghalensis)

　BIRDS OF INDIA

This bird tends to hop along quietly through the bushes of gardens or reeds by streams as well as moist grassland and scrub while feeding on insects. In the past, referred to as a Wren-warbler. Has a distinctive '*jimmy- jimmy-jimmy-jimmy!*' call. *Stewarti* with a white stripe over the eye, is a sub-species.

A widespread breeding resident.

stewarti

Plain Prinia
Prinia inornata

Sada Dum Phudki

Inhabits similar but drier environments than the Ashy Prinia, surviving on a diet of insects such as caterpillars, ants and small beetles as well as flower-nectar. Utters a variety of sounds, notably a plaintive '*tee tee tee*' and a '*kink kink*' and a '*chi up*' repeated rapidly several times; also sings a song sounding like a grasshopper's '*tlick, tlick*' lasting for up to ten seconds at a time. Waves its tail around in typical Prinia fashion.

A widespread breeding resident, not seen in Higher Himalayas or west of Pakistan.

Zitting Cisticola
Cisticola juncidis

10 cms
Jitjitee Jitphudki

breeding

non-breeding

A bird of the grassland, reed-beds near marshes, ditches and standing cereal crops. A skulker that is also a busy bird found in groups. If flushed, it will fly a short distance before disappearing into the grass again. The flight is distinctive as the bird moves upwards in a zig-zag fashion with a fan-shaped tail while emitting a '*zit-zit-zit*' sound similar to a barber's scissors. The nest is a finely constructed pouch that hangs suspended between different grass stems.

Found throughout the region but not so commonly in the north-west.

Oriental White Eye   10 cms
Zosterops palpebrosus   **Poorvi**

Both a local resident and migratory, White Eye is arboreal and can be found in relatively small flocks of about five to 20, hunting for insects amidst the foliage of trees and bushes. Never staying still for very long, clinging to twigs while hanging upside down and poking its beak into nooks and crannies in search of food. Consumes the flesh of fruits and berries as well as the nectar of flowers. The call is a quiet conversational jingle although males during the breeding season deliver a pleasant, tinkling song — initially barely audible yet rising gradually in volume before fading.

Found throughout the region.

Clamorous Reed Warbler (Indian Reed Warbler)   19 cms
Acrocephalus stentoreus   **Bari Narul Phudkee**

Inhabits reed-beds and tall bushes close to lakes, ponds, rivers and swamps. Can be seen alone or in pairs, moving about, often skulking yet occasionally visible; it eats grasshoppers and other insects. The call is a loud and harsh '*chur-r, chur-r*'!

A winter visitor to the region, though occasionally a breeding resident.

Common Tailorbird   13 cms
Orthotomus sutorius   **Samanya Darjin**

Seen in the shrubbery of gardens, singly or in pairs, this little bird is not afraid of human habitation. Can also be seen in jungle areas and hunts for tiny insects including their eggs and grubs as well as flower-nectar. Derives its name from the intricate nests it stitches together, breeding between April and September. Can be found in most places except for the higher mountain reaches and desert areas.

A widespread breeding resident.

Yellow-eyed Babbler
Chrysomma sinense

18 cms
Sonachasm Charkhee

Inhabits thorny scrub and grass jungle as well as reeds and similar vegetation, moving in small groups of about five to 15, skilfully weaving its way through undergrowth in search of spiders and insects although it also eats berries and flower-nectar. Tends to skulk and when disturbed, with an ability to almost vanish, uttering harsh tittering notes as it does so. The call is a loud '*cheep-cheep-cheep*!'

A breeding resident found throughout the region.

Common Babbler
Turdoides caudatus

22 cms
Doomaree Gaugai Charkhee

Prefers dry open country and semi-desert with partial vegetation in the form of thorny bushes and scrubs; yet has been also found in other habitats. This bird feeds from the ground, scuttling around in search of food rather than taking to the wing. The diet comprises insects, berries, grain and nectar from flowers.

Commonly seen throughout the region, it is not seen in the east.

Jungle Babbler
Turdoides striatus

25 cms
Jungli Gaugai Charkhee

A sociable creature, often banding together with others of its flock to ward off danger. This Babbler can be seen on the edges of jungles, well-wooded areas and gardens or where trees are abundant. Keeps up a constant chatter and its diet includes insects such as spiders and cockroaches as well as small fruits and flower-nectar.

Widespread breeding resident.

Indian Bushlark
Mirafra erythroptera

14 cms
Chutdum Iar-bharat

From a bush-top perch, this bird flutters skywards to a height of about 10 metres or so to utter its distinctive call, a mousy '*si-si-si-si*!' followed by a squeaky '*wisee-wisee-wisee*!' which slowly fades as the bird parachutes back to its perch; the wings are kept stiffly outstretched in a wide V-shape above the back while the legs dangle loose. The whole performance lasts about 20 seconds and during the breeding season is repeated over and over again. The chestnut wing patch is distinctive.

Found mainly in central to north India as also elsewhere.

Ashy-crowned Sparrow Lark
Eremopterix grisea

13 cms
Sileti Sir Dabakchiree

male

Inhabits open cultivated country and semi-barren wasteland, standing in a squatting posture on the ground and shuffling along in a zig-zag fashion while searching for seeds and insects. The species displays a noticeable characteristic in the flight dance of the male, who can be seen taking off vertically with quivering wings only to nosedive with wings folded at the sides, after which he suddenly turns to face the sky again — a movement repeated until eventually the bird alights once more on the ground. Eats insects and seeds lying on the ground.

Found through much of the region.

female

Oriental Skylark   16 cms
Alauda gulgula   **Chota Bharat**

A bird found in grassy meadows and on areas of open cultivation in both the hills and on the plains. Prefers damp grassland bordering *jheel*, feeding on seeds and insects. The fluttering flight is distinctive. The bird sings melodiously while in the sky, rising higher and higher after lifting vertically from the ground.

Found throughout the region; a summer visitor to the far north.

Purple Sunbird
Nectarina asiatica

10 cms
Baingani Shakkar Khora

breeding male

displaying male

Found in a variety of habitats such as gardens, among trees, and in cultivated as well as scrub country. Eats insects, spiders, also nectar from flowers for which its curved bill is adept in acquiring; this method of feeding leads to cross-pollination. The bird's call is sharp and monosyllabic although that of breeding males is an excited '*cheewit! cheewit!*' uttered while displaying. Moves singly, in pairs or in groups.

Found throughout the region; a summer visitor to the north-west.

female

male in eclipse plumage

Purple-rumped Sunbird
Nectarinia zeylonica

10 cms
Bara Pachrangee Shakkarkhora

male

Found in the plains, foothills and scrub country, eats insects and fruit, the latter trait making it something of a pest. Found in pairs, breeding all the year round yet favouring the monsoon. Both the sexes contribute to the construction of a pear-shaped nest that hangs suspended. The call is high and thin with an even tempo.

Found in south and central India and in the east.

male

female

House Sparrow   15 cms
Passer domesticus   **Ghareloo Gauraiya**

male

A bird that hangs around human habitation both in the country and the city; it is omnivorous liking grain, insects, fruit-buds and flower-nectar. Can be a nuisance to farmers when it gathers in great numbers to feed on ripening crops.

A breeding resident found throughout the region; a summer visitor to the north.

female

juvenile

Chestnut-shouldered Petronia (Yellow-throated Sparrow)   14 cms
Petronia xanthocollistt   **Lal Kandha Gauraiya**

male

Found in close proximity to human habitation but not so common or attached to man as the House Sparrow, this Petronia likes open scrub country and light deciduous forest. Eats grains and seeds from fields and tracks also berries, flower-nectar as well as insects such as moths. Seen in large flocks during winter months, it sings a chirpy song that is a little sweeter than that of the House Sparrow. Breeds in tree-holes.

Found throughout the region; a summer visitor to Pakistan but not seen in the east.

female

White Wagtail
Motacilla alba

18 cms
Safed Khanjan Dhoban

dukhensis

Running swiftly about with tail constantly wagging, searching for tiny insects on cultivated land as well as in lawns or those inside busy towns. At night it roosts in large colonies along with other Wagtails and Swallows as is obvious from its presence in reed-beds, fields and leaf-covered trees. There are several sub-species with both grey and black-coloured backs.

A winter visitor to most of the region; a summer visitor to the far north.

leucopsis

alboides

personata

White-browed Wagtail
Motacilla maderaspatensis

21 cms
Safed Bhohon Khanjan

male

Inhabits clear, shingly or rocky smooth-running streams with grass growing nearby. Also found near village ponds and large reservoirs; can be quite tame. Lets out a variety of whistling calls yet sings sweetly during the breeding season. A breeding resident, unlike other wintering Wagtails with which it shares a similar diet.

Found throughout the region.

female

Yellow Wagtail
Motacilla flava

17 cms
Pilkiya Khanjan

non breeding (thunbergii)

Having similar habits to other Wagtails, running about in short spurts looking for small insects with occasional flights into the air to catch passing prey. The flight is undulating and often accompanied by a '*weesp!*' call. Roosts in reed-beds and cultivated fields, often flying a long way to feed. There are several sub-species.

A winter visitor to most of the region.

female

male (beema)

A bird of the ground found in open country, plains and hills up to a height of 2,000 metres, it is commonly seen in cultivated fields and grass-covered stony hillsides. Lives on a diet of small insects such as weevils. An upright walker, wagging its tail at a much slower rate than the Wagtail. The male of the species has the habit of flying low over grass with his wings quivering.

A breeding resident found throughout the region.

Streaked Weaver
Ploceus manyar

15 cms
Teliya Baya

breeding male

breeding female

Although very gregarious, this Weaver and its kin build nests that are well spaced with short entrance tunnels, the main part of the nest being a somewhat untidy, woven ball attached to a reed. Flocks emit a shrill chatter '*chit-chit-chit*' while the breeding male sings its own pretty song that can be heard when he is courting a female and inviting her to an available nest. Likes tall grassland and swampy reed margins near water.

Found through much of the region yet absent from many areas.

Baya Weaver   15 cms
Ploceus philippinus   **Samanya Baya**

male

The Baya Weaver is discernible due to its intricate nest often found clustered in considerable numbers, made of woven grass complete with a lower and upper-storey, designed to thwart the efforts of robber Crows and other predators who come looking for eggs and the young. The larger birds cannot hang on to the flimsy nests neither can they easily destroy them although casualties are often high among the Baya Weaver birds. The bird is damaging to crops.

Found in most of the region.

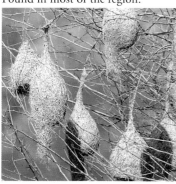

female

breeding male

A Munia that favours damp localities and can be seen in groups. Usually nests during the monsoon, building a ball-shaped structure with a side-entrance found low in a bush or in reeds over water. Their call is a feeble yet musical '*chirrup*!'.

Found in most of the region.

juvenile

Indian Silverbill
Lonchura malabarica

10 cms
Sada Muniya

copulating couple

Found in dry, open country, cultivated as well as uncultivated, sparse scrub and bush land, avoiding humid areas. Formerly known as Munia (white-throated), it shares many characteristics with other Munia, feeding on grain and seeds. Sometimes lays its eggs in the deserted nests of Baya Weaver birds.

A breeding resident found in most parts of the region.

non-breeding

adult: life size

This small bird flies in flocks that might number half a dozen or so but can also be as many as a couple of hundred. They can be seen clinging tenaciously to reeds and larger grasses, yet may fly up into trees or into bushes if disturbed. The diet comprises grass seed and similar products, but may also include insect life.

Found throughout the region but not in the north-west.

sub-adult

juvenile

Common Rosefinch
Carpodacus erythrinus

15 cms
Samanya Laltuti

male approaching breeding; revealing pollen stains

Found in flocks amidst well-wooded country where it lives off berries, wild figs, flower buds, bamboo seeds, linseed and cereals. Cross-pollinates flowers. The call is a musical whistle '*tooee! tooee!*' The nest is a grass and twig-cup placed in a bush.

Found in most of the region; a winter migrant in the south and a summer breeder in the mountainous north.

female

breeding male

ABOUT BIRD WATCHING

"Patience is a virtue!"

If one wants to see birds, the chances are one only has to look out of the window. There may be nothing more spectacular than a few House Sparrows or some noisy cawing Crows yet their behaviour may be interesting to observe. Sparrows tend to be acting out dramas among themselves while Crows are usually up to something, often the bullying of other birds, not only those smaller but also those much larger, whom they will mob in groups. Ornithology is still concerned with the behaviour of such birds whose activities and social structure is by no means a closed book.

The first bird watching aid one might consider is a pair of binoculars as these help to see details that might otherwise be overlooked. The particular plumage of a bird for instance, as well as what they might be carrying in their beak; food or nesting material, possibly an offering of some kind for their mate. Binoculars vary enormously in cost and one will buy according to one's budget yet one needs to also buy a pair suitable for bird watching and these would include a factor such as 8 by 24.

There are of course special places for watching birds such as parks and wildlife sanctuaries (see opposite) where different kinds of bird may more easily be seen. The locations mentioned here are ones that are known to the author and were used in the making of this book. For more information on this subject, there are books available (see bibliography) as well as relevant internet sites. Do not however expect to see all the birds that such books mention as environments change with time and there is a gradual deterioration in bird numbers in the sub-continent as the human population grows and urban sprawl encroaches onto wildlife areas.

The internet is a rich source of information not necessarily accurate, yet one can usually find something that will suggest and describe an area one might want to visit. There may even be a trip report by someone who has been there and can advise on basic logistics. Email forums also exist for certain areas.

Many wildlife parks offer basic amenities such as a canteen and toilets as well as guides. One should remember that these guides are highly unlikely to be ornithologists and while they are very helpful in guiding visitors to the best places to see birds and are often able to rattle off an array of names, these might not always be the right ones.

There are many places where one can see birds in the Indian subcontinent; in fact, bird life is almost everywhere. However, certain designated areas do exist where one is more likely to see a wider range of species. The map above shows the places where most of the birds in this book were photographed and are all parks of some kind or another. For instance, Osho Teerth Park was built at the begining of the 1990's and has a species list of about 50 different birds although it was not intended for avian life. Bharatpur (also known as Keoladeo National Park) was originally constructed as a hunting and shooting place by the Maharaja of Bharatpur; not long after Independence, it became a National Park and has a species list of about 500 birds. Kaziranga in Assam became a National Park at the begining of the 20th century to protect the one-horned rhinoceros and also has a species list of about 500 birds. More details are given in books such as *Important Bird Areas in India* (Islam, Rahmani) published by Birdlife Intl.

Bird photography is far from easy and requires some basic photographic knowledge if you want reasonable results. When I started, my equipment consisted of a film based SLR camera, fast film and a 600mm mirror lens that was reasonably cheap and lightweight but had a fixed aperture of f8; the results were good enough for a magazine. After awhile, I advertised for a second hand, long telephoto lens and ended up buying a 1000mm that needed tripod support so that often the bird would be gone by the time one had set up! However, this system produced some good photos such as that of the Steppe Eagle on page 73. With the advent of digital SLR cameras, bird photography changed dramatically and it was now easier to get closer to birds owing to the increased focal power of the cameras. As well as buying a digital camera, my equipment changed to a more manageable 500mm lens with an extender. Of course, digital photography is only possible with software skills as one usually has to download images from the camera and then process them for printing or viewing onscreen. However, with the appropriate skills, one is much better poised to make recognisable photographs of birds than one was a decade or so ago.

The golden rule is not to compromise the birds one is viewing. One may have travelled many miles to see a particular bird but if it fails to respond to calls and does not want to come out of the undergrowth then leave it. One has at least learnt something about the behaviour of that bird!

There are support groups for birdwatchers where one can meet others and learn more about birding. For some, it may become a hobby and a recreational activity. Wildlife preservation is born out of a love and respect for nature.

BIBLIOGRAPHY

There are numerous books available on Indian Birds. The ones used in the making of this book were:

Birds of the Indian Subcontinent by Richard Grimmett, Carol Inskipp and Tim Inskipp: 1999
(available in both encyclopaedic and handbook form).

Birds of India by Salim Ali: 12'th edition 1996
(although now superseded by recent research and publications, this still remains an excellent and original bird guide).

Birds of India and Nepal by Bikram Grewal: 1995 revised 2003
(a photographic book with smaller photos than the present volume yet covering many more species).

Popular Handbook of Indian Birds by Hugh Whistler: 1928
(from the Colonial Era; republished during the 1960's).

The Life of Birds by Sir David Attenborough: 1998
(almost everything you wanted to know about birds).

Enjoying Birds by Ranjit Lal: 1998
(an enjoyable account by an experienced birdwatcher also illustrated with photographs).

Birds of India by Martin Woodcock: 1980
(a nicely illustrated book about the major Indian birds; published by Collins).

A Birdwatchers' Guide to India: 1998 by Krys Kazmierczak and Raj Singh
(an instructive account of where to find birds in India; Krys's field guide is also an invaluable book).

Birds of South Asia (The Ripley Guide) 2005 by P. Rasmussen and J. Anderton
(a recent and important book about Indian birds in 2 volumes).

BIRDS ON THE INTERNET

There is a virtually inexhaustible source of information about birds, not always correct, available to anyone with a computer that is connected to the Internet. Addresses change but here are a few websites that might be of interest…

Birding in India
http://www.birding.in/

Bombay natural History Society
http://www.bnhs.org/

Sanctuary magazine
http://www.sanctuaryasia.com/

WWF India
http://www.wwfindia.org/

Oriental Bird Club
http://www.orientalbirdclub.org/

Vivek Tiwari's bird pages (useful information on birding trips)
http://www.ee.princeton.edu/~vivek/indian-birds.html

Indian Birds checklist
http://www.ee.princeton.edu/~vivek/indbird.html

A personal website about birding in India
http://www.indiabirds.com/

World Bird Links
http://www.bsc-eoc.org/links/

Biodiversity profile of India
http://www.wcmc.org.uk/igcmc/main.html

About the Indian Environment
http://indianenvironmentonline.net

India Bird Records
http://www.angelfire.com/fl/indianbirds/

Regional sources…

Northern India bird network
http://www.delhibird.org/

Bombay Birds
http://groups.yahoo.com/group/birdsofbombay

Bangalore Birds
http://groups.yahoo.com/group/bngbirds

Birds of Karnataka
http://karnatakabirds.homestead.com/home.html

Birds of Kolkata
http://www.kolkatabirds.com/

Birds of Kerala
http://www.keralabirds.com

Birds of Kashmir
http://www.birdsofkashmir.com/

Basic information about India's wildlife parks all of which are potential birding areas can be found through the United Nations List of National Parks and Protected Areas for India at…

http://www.wcmc.org.uk/

..and more specifically at…

http://www.unep-wcmc.org/igcmc/parks/un93.html

Guidelines for nature photographers

http://www.rps.org/groups/na_code.html

(this site refers to UK laws; Indian ones are similar)

INDEX

INDEX

THE EGGYLOGUE

Male, Red Junglefowl (*Gallus gallus*), **Jungli Murghi**

"Which came first? The chicken or the egg?"

Many find this question unanswerable assuming that the egg referred to must be a chicken's egg! In fact, chickens have been around only for thousands of years…the egg has been around for millions of years before the arrival of the first birds about 150 million years ago! Dinosaurs from whom birds have evolved laid eggs.

So the answer is "The egg!"